LOVING

LONGING

and other

LIMINAL

SPACES

KELLY
PEACOCK

**THOUGHT
CATALOG**
Books

THOUGHTCATALOG.COM

THOUGHT
CATALOG
Books

Published by Thought Catalog Books, an imprint of Thought Catalog, a digital magazine owned and operated by The Thought & Expression Co. Inc., an independent media organization founded in 2010 and based in the United States of America. For stocking inquiries, contact stockists@shopcatalog.com.

Produced by Chris Lavergne and Noelle Beams
Art direction and design by KJ Parish
Creative editorial direction by Brianna Wiest
Circulation management by Isidoros Karamitopoulos

thoughtcatalog.com | shopcatalog.com

First Edition, Limited Edition Pressing
Printed in the United States of America.

ISBN 978-1-949759-79-2

This is for the ones who are navigating
the space of loving and healing
and are learning how to come home to themselves.
This is for the ones who don't know much about love
but know a lot about giving and grieving it.
This is for the ones who are learning
to love themselves instead.

loving and longing.

I do believe it is better to have loved and lost
than to have not loved at all,
but then I think of him
and the way we forfeited our story.
There's nothing poetic about that.

This is what loving looks like.
Loving, longing, loving, losing—
it's all the same
to me.

All I've ever known is loving someone
with mouths agape, arms outstretched,
gently envious of everyone
who comes close to them.
But loving someone and then losing them—
I don't know how to navigate that space.
All I know is that it feels like abandonment.

There is nothing poetic
about the way we
lost one another.

All I want is to not think of you anymore
and how you loved me—
hardly.

I catch myself reaching for you in the dark,
as if you're still next to me under the covers,
as if our legs are still touching,
as if my hair was still getting caught under your arm.
I reach for you,
because that's all I've ever known how to do.

But I am in the middle of the bed now,
under the covers,
in the dark,
and you are not here with me.
You are not reaching back.

We moved together
with such ease,
and purpose,
as if this was supposed to happen for us.
We came together
and let each other go
and then came back together again.
That's the way it goes with twin flames,
wouldn't you agree?
Wouldn't you say this was meant to happen to us?

Not for a lack of trying,
I cannot push the crux of you out of my mind.
The memories I have of you—of us—
are scattered like birdseed,
deepening,
rooting,
and burying themselves.
With each passing day,
you are becoming
someone I desperately want to forget.

It was a slow burn, that clarity:
how the love he gave me just wasn't enough.
It was only ever careless effort,
cruel almosts,
and a longing for more, more, more.

It was only ever
careless effort,
cruel almosts,
and a longing
for more,
more,
more.

If you keep allowing a person into your life
who doesn't properly fulfill your needs,
who doesn't love with white-hot passion,
who doesn't cherish you for all that you're worth,
then this is not the person for you.
There's no reason to surrender
to a closeness you're uncertain about,
especially when you know—in your gut—
there is something so much greater
out there waiting for you.

A love that's like
feeling the sun on your face
for the first time all winter—
that's the love for me.

I don't know what's more wounding:
watching someone you love become
someone you no longer know
or finally understanding they always were
someone you never fully knew at all.

I am trudging through wet sand
as if I have no other choice.
Long distance has a sinking feeling to it,
wouldn't you agree?

They say that home can feel like a person,
and that love should feel like crawling
into bed after a long day.
But why don't we feel like that?
Why does it feel like we are bracing ourselves
for the windows to be smashed in,
for the stovetop to go up in flames,
for the door to slam shut?
Why do I already feel you leaving,
before you've even said goodbye?

I watch our love unravel
and all I can do is hang on by a thread.

Even without him to show me,
I know that love can still feel
like hearing a hum in a silent room.
I know that
a love like what I once had can still exist—
and it does.
I have to have faith in that.

I wonder what it would be like
if we ever saw each other again—
Would you tell me you missed me
and our moments together?
Would you apologize
for everything you never did?

Traitor, I think,
seeing him for the first time in a long time
and with someone else.
It's almost like he can read my mind:
I think I see him look at me,
just before he squeezes her hand tighter.

I don't know if I will ever forgive you
for not loving me in the way I could hold.
But to be honest,
I don't know if I'll ever forgive myself
for doing that too.

We are in a dark bar
when we see each other for the first time
in a long time.
The air between us is thick
and the anxiety is paralyzing.
It's the fear of not knowing
what is going to happen,
if either of us is going to say anything,
and if we do,
what's going to be said.

I have tucked away pieces of you
for safekeeping
and they will stay there
for as long as I let them.
For as long as I want them.

I have tucked away
pieces of you
for safekeeping
and they will stay there
for as long as I let them,
for as long as I want them.

Between you and me,
it was give and take.
I was shamelessly willing for you,
and you were so carelessly cruel
with the way you held it all.
Did you even notice how little you tried,
how little you cared to give?

You never realized how different we were:
to you, our ending was a sad loss,
but for me, it was the end of the world.

There I was, starry-eyed, enamored with you.
I couldn't even see how untouchable you really were,
with your hollowed-out eyes
and your outstretched hands,
waiting for something more worthwhile
to come into your orbit,
as if I wasn't enough,
as if I wasn't a heavenly body worth praising.

It's a lot like pulling teeth—
seeing someone you used to love
and knowing neither of you will say a word.
I'd like to think
there are things we've been meaning to say
to one another,
but maybe it's just me.
Maybe it's just my caring too much
that makes me feel this yearning
for something that used to be.

You gave so little,
but so gingerly,
and I took it and held it close.
Maybe that's how he loves,
I convinced myself.
Maybe this is what I deserve,
I lied.

I used to think that love was about the simple, mundane moments: Sunday mornings on the couch with my legs on top of his, him running into the grocery store across the street to get last-minute ingredients for dinner, falling asleep slowly and entwined in each other's arms.

Love is about looking each other in the eyes and sensing something greater than settling. Love is about holding them close and feeling more than just your bodies touching. Love is more than attachment. Love is more than saying *I love you* for the first time, but softly in another room. Love isn't something you keep quiet about.

But what do I know, really?

It's a complex kind of ache—
feeling grateful for the scarce love he gave me,
but regretting it too.

They say that people love you the best way they know how. This isn't an excuse, but rather an acceptance that maybe he did love me but not in the way I desired.

It's suffocating to remember
how I was so afraid of letting him go,
I took the little indications—never
any ardent utterances—
that he gave me and held on for dear life.

Sometimes people don't love the way you love
Sometimes people can't give the way you give.

Here are some tough pills to swallow:
Sometimes, people don't love the way you love.
Sometimes, people can't give the way you give.

The thing is,
I always knew it was obvious
how much more I cared.
I always knew this
and yet I couldn't get myself
to let go,
to walk away.
Was I just complacent too?

I envy everyone who has never felt
what it was like to love you.

I was so afraid of you leaving me
I didn't even notice how I left myself already;
how I gave so much of myself to you and only you
that I didn't even notice I had spread myself so thin
I became almost nothing.

I loved you way more than I ever loved myself—
and what a tragedy that was.

I hope he lays awake at night and wonders about me.
I hope he thinks of my hands,
my hair, the way I said his name.
I hope he thinks of all the ways
he could've loved me better.
I hope he wonders what I am doing and who I am with.
I hope he thinks of me and it brings him to his knees.

It's such a guttural realization:
I pour out all my love to others
and never save any of it for me.

A part of me wants to pretend
we never mattered to one another,
to let you go,
to pack you up and send you on your way
without a second thought,
much like you did with me.
I want to act as if it wasn't devastating.
I want to walk on our street and not remember
all the times we came here,
palms touching and fingers intertwining.
But the other part of me
will never think that way.
I will never know what it's like
to go somewhere and not think of you.

You lapped it up,
just how much I loved you.
How furiously I let myself melt into you.
I let you take every piece of me
as if I wasn't starved.

I am so tired of love being about bending and breaking,
something I give but never get in return.
I am so tired of love being a vague yearning.

We never admitted to one another:
how we were forcing something out of convenience.
We never had to convince ourselves
we had something certain,
something worth holding on to
in the palm of our hands.
It was almost as if we knew our fate,
our binding break.
We were merely at elbows length,
quietly waiting for it all to fall apart.

losing and grieving.

You look at grief the way people look at stars,
someone tells me,
and I can't help but think of you
and the way we lost each other.

How effortless it was for us:
coming together and parting just the same.
How easy it was,
becoming strangers again.
All we had to do was stay distant
and keep our thoughts and fears and hands to ourselves,
until we were no longer forced to,
until our breaking became somewhat bearable.
I am still mourning our togetherness
and I think a part of me always will.

When we fell apart officially
it felt like we finally reached that point of no return—
acceptance that this was going nowhere further.
But where do we go from here?
Where do I go from here?
I guess all I can do is try to navigate this new space,
to let myself feel empty and lost
if that's what I feel.
(It is what I feel.)

I am still mourning
our togetherness
and a part of me
always will.

This is the most agonizing kind of ending—
surrendering to the inevitable of
having to let each other go,
and watching our love go with it.
This undoing was bound to happen,
simply because that's just the way things go sometimes,
when love just isn't built to last.

I often think about the last time I saw you,
how I didn't savor our closeness for all it was worth.
Do you think about this too?
Do you wonder what it would've felt like
if we held onto each other a little bit longer?

"you look at grief the way
people look at stars."

I can't help but think
of you and the way
we lost each other.

It's okay to be in denial,
to want things to go back to the way they were,
to miss them, their hands, their smell.
But please don't wait around for them.
Don't hold out for a grand gesture
or a despairing apologetic moment.
Don't contradict your heart and neglect your truth
by wanting a reconciliation.
Please remember that
you are not meant to be with this person.
You have to let them go.

It snags you like a thread,
every thought
that doesn't matter,
every despairing question that cuts
and extends to the forefront of your mind,
making a home next to your memories
and your self-doubt:
Why did I bind myself to him for so long?
Was I enough?

Grief hits me out of nowhere—on the subway, in the shower, falling asleep, opening a window, making coffee in the morning. Every ounce of my body succumbs to it. Every part of me misses him, and I am desperate to tell him how much I do as if that would change anything about where we are now. But this is not something that needs to be said. We know that we miss one another, but there's nothing that can be done about that. We have to keep our "I miss yous" and "thinking of yous" to ourselves. We have to walk through this door, this closure, on our own. We are no longer together, and that's something we have to learn to live with.

Are you hurting too?
Or are you just better at pushing it away?
Maybe, even after things ended,
I was still the one who cared more,
who loved more, who ached more.
That says a lot more about you than me,
wouldn't you agree?

We are in limbo—
loving yet leaving
grasping and grieving.
I am having a hard time believing that
anything we do or say will make any of this easier.

I wonder if he misses me half as much as I miss him.

I wonder if he notices my absence at all.

Maybe I'll never know
if you felt anything about our demise,
if our parting ever made you ache,
if remembering me felt like pouring salt in a wound.
Maybe I'll never know how you felt
and I'll spend the rest of my life
wondering,
hoping it brought you to your knees, too.

When I think of us,
I think of expiration dates.
We saw the signs, our faults.
And yet, we still tried. We still loved.
I think of that last week we spent together,
the knowing of what was to come
hanging over our heads.

I couldn't help but notice the difference between us:
I sat with discomfort in my chest,
a pit in my stomach,
a tightness in my throat,
and he went on his way
without any agony,
without any what-ifs looming.
It's crushing to think
I'm alone in this heaviness.

Maybe it makes me the heartless one
that I want him to feel an indescribable emptiness,
to feel that lump in the throat,
to wake up in a sweat and think of me.
It's too lonely,
too burdening,
too exhausting
to be the only one this distraught.

Are you missing me yet?

Wondering this in the first place
tells me all I need to know.

I talk about it because I want to make sense of it: the paralysis of accepting the fate of a relationship, mourning a person who is still alive. It's lonely, reaching the aftermath of the end: the disenfranchised grief, watching the world carry on and expecting me to do the same. *No one is paying attention to my ache.*

I want to talk about it all, the layers to the desolation, the death of my identity, the becoming of someone new without him. *Doesn't anyone know what this feels like?* There's only so much I can say to someone who is willing to listen to me before it becomes too trying, before they tell me how they can't hold my grief. *I don't expect you to say anything that would make me feel better.*

I know I don't have to talk about it. I don't have to make sense of these gutless feelings. I simply have to accept where and who I am, even if that means feeling the weight of being lost and navigating a new, quiet space.

Every time I hear your name,
I hold my breath.
It's as if holding it long enough
could convince the Universe
to bring you back to me
and let me hold on to you
this time around.

When you finally realize you have to let them go, you will deny it. There will be bartering with the Universe, a chorus of what-ifs, desperate attempts to try and make this love work. You will do everything in your power to keep each other close: you'll remain in touch, asking how their days are, talking about the shows you used to watch together but are now watching alone, forcing a connection.

Eventually, though, your hands will become calloused from hanging on too tightly to something, someone that isn't yours to keep. And when you finally pry your hands away from the hope you can fix it, you might feel nothing at first. There won't be any agonizing ache yet. There's just numbness. There's dissociation.

One day it will come, though. The grief. This gnawing will be so intense and so consuming and it just might be unlike any other hopelessness you've felt before. The misery will hit you out of nowhere: opening a window, in the shower, in the car, on a train, in the grocery store. You will find yourself crying often. You will start to feel the anger swelling in your throat, too—the resentment, the desperation to make sense of why this all had to happen.

Eventually, you will begin moving toward acceptance. You will start to make coffee for one. You will learn to fall asleep in the middle of the bed. You will have to stop yourself from calling them when you have news, when you're bored, when you're on your way home, when you just want to hear their voice. You will have to create a new space and hide reminders of them, like photos and t-shirts. You will remove their friends and family from your life, just as they're probably doing too. You will realize how lonely this all is. You will keep moving forward despite all the empty spaces.

In time, you will throw up your hands and surrender. You will accept your fate for what it is.

Maybe there was friction.
Maybe there was loneliness.
Maybe your love for one another
just wasn't enough for the long distance.
Whatever the reason,
there is nothing tender
about letting go of someone you love,
even if you have to,
even if it's for the best.

There is nothing tender
about letting go of
someone you love,
even if you have to,
even if it's for the best.

I don't mean to romanticize my grief,
but this is all I know how to do.
This is how I make sense of it.
This is how I let him go.

One day the weight of loving you
and missing you will let up.
One day I will feel relief.

Sometimes I get so lost in my heartsickness
that I don't know anything else exists.
There is no ill will, no revenge.
I so badly wish I could feel something
other than this lonely misery.
I so badly wish I felt less empty
and more full of anger.

This is the nature of grief,
my therapist tells me,
you've tapped the well.
I am finally feeling everything
I've been ignoring for so long.
I am drowning
in my heartache,
mourning a person still alive.
The water is so heavy.
I want to float.
I want to feel light.
But the current of despair keeps pulling me
under.

In the beginning,
I thought he was one of the good ones
and the way he loved me
was sweet like cherry wine.
Maybe it's because he loved me differently—
maybe even better—
than the ones who came before him.
With him, there was no malevolence, no ill intentions.
But there was no grace, either.
Now, with every passing day,
my belief in him dissipates.
Through all of my fury,
I can see it for what it really was,
how he only kept me close for the hell of it.
Now, there is no redemption arc for him.
There are no sins to confess,
he is simply not as holy as I once believed.
He is just a man.
The wine was always water.

I have no say in the matter—
I have to feel my suffering
until it fades.

I hold too much space for my sadness.
My deep grief, my ache,
my homesickness for someone—anyone.
I don't know how to make room for anything else.

It's such a tragedy, coming to terms with the fact that the person you once loved has become a stranger again.

I need to forgive myself for making a home for my sorrow. For letting my heartbreak become a part of me, like chipped paint. I need to forgive myself for the fact that I don't know how to let things go, even long after they have left, even after they've served a purpose. I need to forgive myself for the way I never see how I make space for my hurt until it becomes like a flickering front porch light and the moths that flutter around it, until it becomes too noticeable to ignore.

How brutal it was,
merely playing the part of lovers,
fighting for a chance.
But eventually, we had to surrender
to our free fall into No Man's Land,
with all its desolation and uncertainty.
We knew we were better off this way;
We knew we had to stop battling.

There is something so unkind about it all:
severing ties with someone who still has your heart.
I wish I could plead with the Universe
and ask her why this was our fate,
why anything worth having is also worth losing.

I wish I could plead with the Universe
and ask her
why this was our fate,
why anything worth having
is also worth losing.

Forgetting the person you once loved is a lot more subtle than you'd think. At first, everything you've ever known about them will take up so much space inside of you. It will be so weighted and so present in your brain: the gracefulness of their breath while they slept, the smell of their cologne, the way their eyes crinkled when they laughed.

But eventually, all of these little things will pass and soon mean nothing. You will start to forget them, and when you do, you won't notice it at first. It will be slow. Discreet. You will soon be unable to recall the pattern of their breath, the shape of their hands, their fragrance. You will forget the moments you shared, the memories you made. You will see it all in a different light: how your parting wasn't tragic, just fate.

Even after all this time,
I still feel haunted by you.
I mean, maybe not you,
but the ghost of someone
who I used to believe loved me.

I don't know much
about love,
but I do know a lot
about grieving it.

I don't know much about love
but I do know a lot about grieving it.
I know the heart aches more at night.
I know that it feels solemn and heavy,
yet empty,
missing what we used to be.
I know how devastating it is
to have to let go of someone you love
who still loves you.
I know that sometimes,
you have no other choice
but to watch them become a silhouette
you no longer recognize.

What a wearying thing it is,
having to love someone
you were always going to lose.

Our initial break was clean.
There were no sharp words thrown,
no sinners,
no would've, could've, should'ves.
You let me go like you had been waiting
for the exact right moment to
and I rushed to acceptance,
to make everything light and unyielding,
to keep myself from feeling
the rectitude of who we really were together.
But now, everything about us is eroding.
It wasn't until I detached completely
I finally saw our frailties,
your carelessness for my heart,
me, willingly handing it over to you.
With each day,
another part of us—
and the love I had for you—
cracks.

grief comes in waves

trying to let go of someone
you've built into a lifeboat
feels like drowning.

I tell people how grief comes in waves,
how trying to let go of someone
you've built into a lifeboat
feels like drowning.

When you finally realize he wasn't the man you thought he was, you will feel it. It's an ache in your chest, your gut, your whole being. Maybe you've felt it before or maybe this is the first time. But this kind of ache will be so heavy, like cupping your hands underwater. You're trying to hold it, but you can't—it's just slipping through the cracks of your fingers. This feeling will consume your body, filling you with hopelessness. Disappointment. Regret. You will become a graveyard of everything you never wanted to feel.

When you realize he wasn't the man you thought he was, you might tell yourself that *you* did something wrong, that *you* were the problem, *you* were the reason he did the things he did. None of that is true. Don't be scared into thinking it was your fault—because it wasn't. If this happens, just be gentle with yourself. That false narrative will disappear eventually. Self-forgiveness isn't easy, but it is necessary. Forgive yourself for not only blaming yourself for what happened, but also for staying with him for longer than you should've, and for accepting the little love he barely gave you.

When you finally realize he wasn't the man you thought he was, you will also realize what and who you deserve. Sometimes it's not easy to see how you're settling for the bare minimum from someone when you're in it. Especially when you love them. Especially when you feel safe and comfortable with them. Especially when you think that's all you're worth, or when you don't realize how much *more* you deserve.

You might also ask for closure from him. You might ask for an apology, or at the very least just wait around for one. But when you realize he wasn't the man you thought he was, you will also have to accept that you might not get closure. You might not get an apology. It's a tough pill to swallow, but you will have to find closure in your own way. That's just the way it goes.

When you realize he wasn't the man you thought he was, you will feel betrayed. You will feel sorry for yourself. You will regret loving him. And all of that is valid. Every feeling you're feeling is valid—and it will eventually pass. It will feel lighter, one day.

When we had to release one another
from our grip,
there was no fighting.
No hunger, no devouring.
We just bit our tongues
and bled.

What does it matter anymore?
What will knowing this do for your healing?
my therapist asks me
after I tell her how badly I wish I knew
how he felt about us now that we're over.

It's not that I want something to change
or for things to go back to the way they were.
Maybe it's just a closure thing.
Maybe I just want to know
if I meant *something* to him,
if my love meant *anything* to him.

I just want to know
if I meant something to him,
if my love meant anything to him.

Even after all this time, I still think about the night we ended things. Your dark living room, only with the glow of the muted TV on our faces. (How come yours was still in the shadow?)

It was the way you held me, and still kept me at a distance. We sat in silence for a long time, letting our hands part. There was so much tension knowing this was over. *So this is it, then?* I asked. (Why was it always me trying?) *I guess so,* was all you could muster up.

There was nothing else we needed to say—we knew this was it for us. We knew that sometimes love fades and two people aren't meant to be with one another. (This is for the best, I know it.)

I wondered, in that moment, if you could sense the empty pit in my stomach and if you felt the same or if you were just better at hiding it.

Sometimes love fades
and two people aren't
meant to be together
anymore.

(This is for the
best, I know it.)

Sometimes I catch myself thinking of him.
I miss his hands, their tightness around mine.
His laugh. His hair in the mornings.
But I don't miss the way he barely loved me,
how he would put his wants and needs first,
or his eyes, never present with mine.
I realize it now,
how missing him just means
I miss having a *him* there at all.

Why did you keep me to yourself?
Why was your love so discreet?
You know I shouldn't have loved you as much as I did, right?

There's so much I want to ask him,
so much I want to tell him,
but he's not worth my breath
anymore.

One day it will feel less like a loss: our inevitable dismantling. One day I will let go of you and all that you were: your cologne, the songs you used to sing in the shower, the way your body twitched as you fell asleep. You will forget me too. You will forget the way I loved you, with so much courage and conviction. One day we will hold each other close—only in our memories—and that will be it for us.

Sometimes you have to let the undoing be what it is.
Gutwrenching. Paralyzing.
Watch it fall apart—
that's what's supposed to happen.
It's not meant for you to mend.
The hardest part is over, he says,
and I believe him.
Every inch of our separation is one step closer
to finding a love that feels like solace,
a homecoming.

feeling and healing.

For so long, my body has been a vessel of self-abandonment. It's not easy for me to admit how badly I ignored myself, and for so long. But I know now how the first step into giving my body the grace it merits is facing that self-inflicted pain. It's about trusting my body. It's about being patient with myself. It's about coming home to myself. It's about the small gestures that say *I love you* better than anyone ever could.

My body has allowed for the
bruising to wilt inside of me
and fester into something dirty,
something worse than the act itself.
I know it's necessary
for me to dig out my pain
with my bare hands
like pulling weeds from their roots.
I know what I need to do to let go,
but I can't.
I can't get myself to look at it,
no matter how crucial,
no matter how demanding.

Is there a part of you
that feels good about who you are?
What do you like about yourself?
my therapist asks me,
and I don't know where to begin.
I look at myself in the mirror and feel detached.
I don't think I like really anything,
I admit.
I don't think I feel at home in my body,
I want to say.

For so long, you've pushed down the heartbreak. You avoided it and drowned it out because that was your way of protecting yourself. It was your way of coping. What you did or didn't do is not something to be mad at yourself for. But you can't keep letting yourself go on with this sense of dread, this baggage that shouldn't be yours to carry.

If you haven't yet healed from your undigested trauma, I want you to know that's okay. But what's not okay is ignoring that internalized bruise. You have to acknowledge it. You have to gently face your pain and let yourself heal slowly.

you have to gently face your pain
and let yourself heal slowly.

My anger has always been merciful,
like the first few raindrops before a storm,
but I want it to be more than that.
I want more than the tidal waves
to hold my entire being hostage.
I want my rage to be a tsunami—
unexpected,
almighty.

You need to keep facing those parts of you that are in need of a little bit more attention. These pieces of you will remain bruised until they are tended to and worked through, like massaging out a sore muscle. You need to knead out the knots, the tender spots, until you feel a release, until you feel like yourself again.

I so badly want to crack open,
to feel free.
I want to know what it feels like
to be at ease.

The way I respond to my trauma is anchored in me,
like muscle memory.
I tighten. I tense.
My body folds in
the same way
I cradle water in my hands.
I so badly want to crack open, to feel free.
I want to know what it feels like to be at ease.

They say to pull weeds from their roots slowly so that you can get the whole thing. So I think of all that I've buried, everything I forced myself to forget. Now I am uprooting, with my bare hands, every moment that made me feel small or as if my needs didn't matter. Finally, I am releasing my grip.

Like a woodpecker to a tree, you have
to keep gnawing at your hurt.
This is the only way you're going to break it all down.
This is the only way you're going to heal.

Healing is about falling apart just as much as it's about *trying not to* fall apart. It's about moving in slow motion, cracking your hands open to release what you once held close. It's about letting yourself feel the hole in your chest, no matter how heavy and excruciating it is. Healing is about feeling lonely. Healing is about trying to remember that the pain won't last forever, even if it feels like it will.

I am tired of getting in the way of my healing,
not being in tune with my bones.
I am tired of inviting the anger
to merely sit at the back of my throat—
waiting to be devoured again.
I am tired of feeling ashamed
for not being able to forgive myself,
for knowing how crucial it is to love myself
but never feeling like I'm doing it right.
I am tired of
mourning who I used to be,
when I so badly just want to let her be free.

Want to know how to put yourself back together?

You put yourself first. You give yourself permission to look at your scars, to recognize your damage. You grieve whatever it is you need to grieve: the person you once were, the way you lost yourself and neglected your needs.

By allowing your body to mold into something you never want to look at, you grow comfortable with the discomfort. You are self-sabotaging yourself and who you are meant to become.

You have to sit in this until you get the urge to make it all better, to want to feel free.

One day you will realize the grieving. You will realize how harsh you are with letting go of your old self, yet how sensitive you are to coming into someone new.

You will realize you are letting go of a person who didn't do something about their hurt and healing because then that would mean having to face it all in the first place. It's denial and you're fighting it for all that it's worth.

But one day, you will realize the necessity of paying attention to it all: your experience, how you reacted to it, and what you're doing about it now.

It might be slow and in small moments or all at once: the shame of what happened, the weight of burying it all in the pit of your stomach, the furiousness of not doing anything about it all sooner.

Although everything you're feeling is valid, I want you to know that you won't be feeling it all forever. It's going to take some time to find solace in where you are in this healing journey, and that's okay. One day it will hit you how badly you need to face it head-on, grieve the person you once were, and let go.

One day you will realize how you've been self-sabotaging: holding yourself back from your necessary growth as a means of protection. Thank your body for protecting you when it needed to, but also give yourself the grace to know when you have to step further into the pain in order to truly heal. You are harming yourself more by letting the trauma sit heavy in your body. You have to release it.

One day you will realize just how necessary it is to face your pain. You have to grieve your old self—the person who was avoidant and in denial. You have to welcome with warm arms someone new, someone who wants to heal and wants to do something about their healing.

One day you will realize how you've been
self-sabotaging: holding yourself back from
your necessary growth as a means of
protection.

Thank your body for protecting you when
it needed to, but also give yourself the
grace to know when you have to step
further into the pain in order to truly
heal. You are harming yourself more by
letting the trauma sit heavy in your
body. You have to release it.

Every morning begs the question,
Will it sting a little less today?
I look at this body and wonder if
this is the day I start to love it,
even if it is broken.
I wonder if I'll ever stop thinking of his hands
on my thighs, my chest, my throat.
Will I ever feel good as I am?
Will I ever look at myself
and not think of what he did to me?

The ghosts you've neglected for so long will be asking something of you: *to face them.* You don't have to accept them or try to understand them. All you have to do is pay attention to them, to all that haunts you: the words you choked on, the way your body recoiled, the hurt done at the hands of another. You have to stop treating this detriment like an afterthought. This is the only way you can release it into the light.

If you don't talk about what weighs you down,
you will just keep storing it.
If you let it make a home inside of you,
it will become too arduous to hold.
If you want to release it,
you have to feel it first.
And then you can let it go.

You cannot continue to avoid the discomfort of your trauma—the verity of the ruin, the feebleness of holding it in your hands—just because you have convinced yourself that it did not leave a mark on you. You cannot continue to push everything down with the hopes that if you ignore it, it will go away.

I often look at my healing as something shameful.
I store it away like a skeleton in the closet,
and I treat my body the same way,
folding in on myself,
and neatly packing away my bones like secrets.
I don't know how to look at myself
as anything more than flesh hanging on bone.
All I know is shrinking.
All I know is breaking.

I don't even feel like a body anymore.
I just feel like a vessel for my scars.

I never know what to say
when someone asks what I did after it happened,
or how I took care of the wound.
All I know is that
I looked at myself in the mirror
and was terrified of the body I was in.
All I remember was sweeping my trauma under the rug
and burying myself under a weighted blanket,
afraid to be seen.

No one really talks about what it's like
to crave intimacy
when you also have a crushing fear of it.
To have a faceless force sit on your chest—
no one really tells you
how suffocating it is.

When you are putting yourself back together, you will often feel defeated by the rebuilding. Every chance you get to feel less like a walking wreckage, something—or someone—comes along and knocks you down.

And you let them.

The next time this happens, force yourself to get back up again. Remind yourself how you no longer want to feel like a broken thing. Stop resisting your necessary growth. Fight for yourself for once.

Because he wants to,
and because I let him,
he puts his hands on my thighs.
Like a fever,
he becomes hot with want
and all I can do is watch it happen.
Detached,
I am letting this be
an out-of-body experience.

No one warned me
how after trauma,
it won't be easy finding peace in my body,
or finding peace in my body *with* his body—
no matter how safe it is,
no matter how badly I want it.

I am crying on the bathroom floor again, letting the agony take hold of the room around me. If I felt okay, I might notice the cold tiles under my feet, hear the shower running, or see the steam fogging up the mirror. But I don't. I am crying on the bathroom floor again and I can't make sense of anything. All I know is that I am here, still suffering.

No one tells you
how your body will betray you
in an effort to protect you,
how your trauma will taint your mind
and your body will crucify you for it.
No one tells you how harsh that realization is—
how you're dying for sins that aren't even yours.

I have forgotten how to unleash my rage,
to let the righteous fury slither across my tongue.
Instead—because it's easier to—
I let it sit and slip back down my throat.

It feels a lot like purgatory,
that somewhere in between space
of knowing one thing and feeling another.
After the leaving, the succumbing, the breaking—
my body did what it needed to do
to protect me:
it tucked the pain away
like a distant memory
and put up walls to keep me safe.
But it's simply adding insult to injury,
letting every bad feeling fester and grow inside of me.
It's a pushing and pulling battleground of
my mind, recognizing that I'm worthy
of healing and forgiveness
while my body still wants to shield me.
It's keeping me from
what I need the most: *healing.*

Something happened to you and you became numb. You stopped feeling. You took your pain inward and banished it to the depths of your mind. You did this as a means of protection. You thought it was an act of self-love, not allowing yourself to feel the reality of what happened. You suppressed the damage and it became dominant.

But let me tell you this: exiling your trauma to the back of your mind will allow it to become a part of you. And it's tender, the way it settles into your body.

You will start to notice the body language of it all, how your spine and your hips tighten and cave in. You fold your arms and tuck your legs to your chest and let yourself become as small as you can be. Your body will become afraid of its own shadow, afraid of the way its darkness takes up space.

The longer you pretend your trauma doesn't exist, the more distant it becomes—but it will also get stronger too. Eventually, this ache will swell. It will take up so much space inside of you that you don't even realize it. And it will become nearly impossible to defeat. It will become louder and it will convince you that what happened and how you dealt with it was your fault.

This is the brutality of it all: you hold yourself back from feeling that pain, despite how crucial it is. You fawn. You tiptoe around it as if your mind is a minefield; you dodge the memories of how it felt when it all happened.

It's complex—the very thing you're afraid of is what you have to face the most. In its own twisted way, this "armor" is self-sabotage; by letting your trauma make a home in your body, you're keeping yourself from true healing.

You have to return to the war. You have to let yourself feel it all: the righteous anger, the quiet grief. Bring the torture to the forefront of your brain and fight it. By confronting it, you can then let it go. Don't let yourself become numb to it forever. Be brave enough to go back to the battlefield and face it head-on. Stare it down until it surrenders. Fight for your healing. Your heart. Yourself. Because you don't really have another choice.

It's complex — the very thing you're afraid of
is what you have to face the most.
In its own twisted way, this "armor"
is self-sabotage: by letting your trauma
make a home in your body, you're keeping
yourself from true healing.

If I'm being honest,
I have been sitting comfortably in
my discomfort for so long,
I don't know what it feels like to not.

One day,
when you least expect it,
you will start to feel it all:
the ugliness of what happened to you,
the heaviness of white-knuckling
it for as long as you did.
It is necessary that you look at these parts of you,
despite how devastating they are.
Forgive yourself
for shoving the trauma into the framework of your being
for as long as you did.
You can hate where you are now,
but you must still accept it.
This is the only way you are going to get better.

More often than not, our bones let the blow crystallize inside of us. And eventually, it hardens. It sinks its teeth into our flesh without mercy. We don't want it or need it, but it stays put anyway, paralyzing us. It so furiously becomes a part of who we are and who we are becoming. We don't even realize how broken down we are until we've withered into someone we no longer recognize.

In its own twisted way, this is our subconscious trying to protect us. Burying the trauma is our refusal to feel the pain and to make sense of what happened. This detachment is still an attachment. The scar is still an open wound. The trauma still exists even if we pretend it does not.

Let yourself be in it.

The only way to heal
is to feel the hurt
in its entirety.

Feel it until it passes.

Let yourself be in it,
my therapist tells me
when I say the grief is all-consuming.
The only way to heal is to feel the hurt in its entirety.
Feel it until it passes.
I know this,
but that doesn't mean it's any more bearable.

coming home.

One day you'll realize it: how, for so long, you've allowed yourself to be small. Graceful. A pleaser. You never took up too much space, never asked for your needs to be met, never let yourself step out of complacency. One day you'll realize all of that, and it will be devastating, the way you broke your own heart. You'll have a hard time forgiving yourself for not respecting yourself enough to be loud, to be wanting, to be here.

One day everything will change. You'll learn what your voice sounds like, what it feels like to take up space. Then, self-forgiveness will come—and it *will* come. You have to trust yourself enough to keep feeling. You have to trust yourself enough to keep healing.

All my life I have tiptoed around my own feelings,
for fear of asking too much,
for fear of not being enough.
I have swallowed my ache
and let it fill my lungs.
But one day, it hit me out of nowhere
and I split myself open.
As if I were standing outside of my body,
I watched myself no longer let things happen to me.
Now I no longer feel like
I'm breathing with a broken rib—
it just feels like breathing.

Is it possible I'll ever stop putting my
worth in the hands of someone else?
And instead of squeezing my meaning
between their fingertips,
they would give it back to me and
not leave me fractured?

In retrospect,
maybe I didn't love you
as much as I thought I did.
Maybe I was elbows-deep in you
like a heavy sweetness
because I didn't think
there was anything else out there for me.
But there is—
there are kinder hearts, tender
pleasure, deeper devotion,
and everything I've always wanted.
I cannot continue settling for anything less.

It's disappointing, really,
seeing it all for what it really was:
how I betrayed myself and my needs
in order to keep the peace,
to keep myself small enough
to fit in his pocket.
I won't be a bother.
I'll just be here.

I wanted to receive love so badly
that I saw the crumbs he gave me as enough.
How unkind I was to myself,
letting this happen to me.
I know this isn't something I can change,
but it is something I can forgive myself for.

It's such a bitter way of living:
being merciful,
for fear of asking for your needs to be met.
Because the thing is,
it is never too much.
The way they loved you just wasn't enough.

the way they loved you
just wasn't enough.

When I think about love,
I think about selflessness.
To me, love has always been about giving.
But I see now how wrong this is,
how selfish that selflessness really was.
What I mean is:
how selfish of me
to give all my love and respect and grace
to someone else,
never leaving any of it for me.

Maybe this is me moving on.

Maybe this is me moving on.

Maybe this is me finally taking off the rose-tinted glasses and seeing our relationship for what it truly was. Attachment. You, loving me only because I was in front of you, and me, loving you only out of fear of not keeping you. You, with one foot out the door, and me, stepping through the frame as if I had no other choice.

But I see it all clearly now, how I *did* have the choice to let you go. I couldn't bear the idea of being the first to leave, but I also couldn't bear the idea of you leaving first, too. So I stayed until life got in the way—as it always does. I accepted the little love you were willing to give, not realizing how truly little it was, not realizing how I am worth so much more than that.

Maybe this is me feeling sorry for myself. Maybe this is me trying to understand why I believed your love was this tender, forever thing when it was actually reserved, lackluster. Why I never asked for more, why I feared being too needy, too much, not enough.

Maybe this is me finally understanding that sometimes love doesn't happen for two people, no matter how badly you want it to. I am accepting the fact that sometimes the love you want isn't the love you deserve or the love you need.

Maybe this is me grieving and finding my own closure. I am letting go of every moment I shared with you and tucking it away to become a distant memory. Maybe moving on is me trying to make sense of our togetherness and our parting and how sad it all was— till the very end.

I'm not calling out your name anymore.
I'm only letting out a sigh of relief.

It's the strangest yet most beautiful feeling in the world:
realizing you finally moved on from
someone you used to love.

It's not easy to admit that
you accepted crumbs
and said it kept you full.
It's not easy to admit that
you stuck to them out of fear.
It's a gutted realization,
but an important one—
you might feel starved,
but at least you'll be free.

I know that I have finally let you go
because I feel a delicate ease.
I feel the weight of
not being loved enough
lifted.
My shoulders have lowered,
my jaw unclenched.
I have let you go,
and finally, I can exhale.
Finally, I can breathe.

how crucial it is
to make a home
in my bones.
how necessary it is
to find solace,
to not let myself
shrink.

It wasn't until his withdrawal—and the echoing of it in my body—that I realized how crucial it is to make a home in my bones. How necessary it is to find solace, to not let myself shrink.

I can't help but feel sad for myself though, knowing that someone's leaving is what makes me finally come home to myself.

I don't know the difference between being jaded
and no longer looking at love
in shades of pink
but I do know that
I am no longer giving out second
and third and fourth chances.
I am no longer letting my desire to be wanted
be greater than my need to be respected.
I am understanding how
I've let people rob me of my kindness
for longer than I should've.
Now, *I* am the one
who chews them up
and spits them out
like a cherry pit,
as if this is something
I've always known how to do.

It was that negligence
I am so ashamed of:
how I kept myself still,
and I let myself shrink,
for fear of being too much
and also not enough.

There are some people in this life you can't help but love so deeply, so fiercely. Sometimes, though, those people are not meant for you to love them. Sometimes, these people are unworthy of you.

Someone who takes advantage of your kindness, who never gives you the space to say when your feelings are battered, who assumes you will always be there for them, who makes you feel small—these people are not meant for you to love. These people often expect and are unappreciative of all that you give—and that's why you have to let them go.

There will be a moment when you realize the way you've been mistreated. You will feel sorry for yourself for not asking yourself, *Is this what I want?* You will feel ashamed for letting yourself accept anything less than you deserved—but you have to forgive yourself. Forgive yourself for getting so lost in it, for abandoning yourself for as long as you did.

You will feel angry, too. You will want revenge in some way—and you might even want them to feel as mad the way you do. But you can't fight fire with fire. You fight by walking away. You fight for *yourself* by walking away.

It's easier said than done, but one day, you will think about them less and less. One day, they will be irrelevant and you will feel indifferent toward them. One day, you will feel solace.

As if I was supposed to, I held onto that innate ache of losing you. I didn't want to let go of my melancholy because that meant I would be letting you go with it, and I wasn't ready for that yet, for a life without you.

But now I am.

I know I'm not meant to keep you any longer. I know I have to release this thread, to cut the rose-colored string. And so I do.

This is me no longer
allowing myself to be palpable,
fearing I take up too much space,
always anchoring my voice.
This is me believing that
I am so much more than someone to merely tolerate.

There is a difference
between giving love and needing reassurance,
my therapist tells me,
and I can't help but think of him.
I think of every man I've ever loved,
how it is such a gentle burden for me
to give so much of myself to them
and for them to give so little in return.
I think of how lonesome it is,
to love someone
simply because I just want them to love me, too.

I'm having a hard time forgiving myself
for being malleable
when I shouldn't have been,
for swallowing my anger
instead of letting it burst,
for carrying my fear
as if I had no other choice.

I often thought about his hands,
his hunger,
and the greedy lick of his fingers.

But I don't think of him
like that anymore.
I don't think of him
as much
or the way I used to.

I believe it to be true, that love can make you a different person. Maybe even leave you better than you were before. I believe the woman I am now—braver, stronger, more attuned to my body and my needs—is because that's who I am at my core. I just needed someone to bring her out of me.

I know that love still exists,
even if it's not coming from him anymore.
(But then again, maybe it never came from him at all.)

I know that love still exists
even if it's not coming from him
anymore.

(But then again,
maybe it never
came from him
at all.)

It's okay if I don't forgive myself yet.
Right now I'm still hurting, and that's okay.
Self-forgiveness is a journey—
For now, I just need to meet myself where I'm at.

It is so goddamn powerful
to let yourself love and be loved again,
even after all the heartbreak
that made you feel unlovable.

Self-forgiveness is a journey.

For now,
I need to meet myself
where I'm at.

To me, love has always been about sacrifice.
I want to know what it's like
to choose myself instead.
I want to know how to quiet the guilt
and make love something I give myself
for once.

end

Kelly Peacock is a New York City-based writer,
poet, and author of *Somewhere In Between*.
This is her second poetry collection.

instagram.com/kellyapeacock

THOUGHT
CATALOG
Books

Thought Catalog Books is a publishing imprint of
Thought Catalog, a digital magazine for thoughtful
storytelling, and is owned and operated by The Thought
& Expression Co. Inc., an independent media group
based in the United States of America. Founded in 2010,
we are committed to helping people become better
communicators and listeners to engender a more exciting,
attentive, and imaginative world. The Thought Catalog
Books imprint connects Thought Catalog's digital-native
roots with our love of traditional book publishing. The
books we publish are designed as beloved art pieces. We
publish work we love. Pioneering an author-first and
holistic approach to book publishing, Thought Catalog
Books has created numerous best-selling print books,
audiobooks, and eBooks that are being translated in over
30 languages.

ThoughtCatalog.com | **Thoughtful Storytelling**

ShopCatalog.com | **Shop Books + Curated Products**